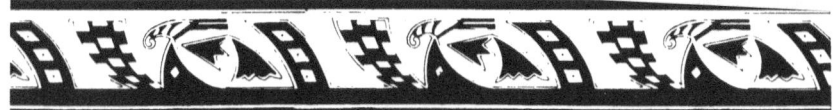

Prehistoric and Historic Pottery of the Southwest

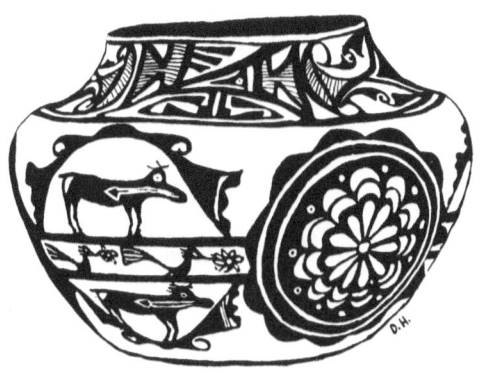

A Bibliography

by

Wm. Farrington

Illustrations by — Ronald Bayford

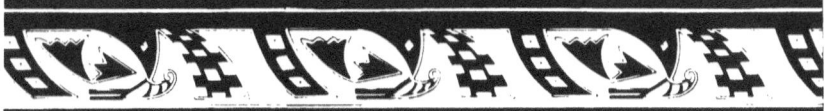

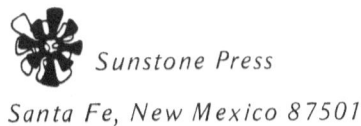

Sunstone Press

Santa Fe, New Mexico 87501

FIRST EDITION

Book and Cover Design: Douglas J. Houston

Printed In The United States of America

ISBN 0-913270-45-8

FOR ROZ ADAMS

INTRODUCTION

This short bibliography was mothered, as is often the case, by necessity. During the past few years Indian arts have come out of the handicraft stage into which they had fallen and have entered the realm of fine arts. Because of this renaissance people have become interested in the history and development of the native arts, and nowhere is this more evident than in ceramics.

When the beginner starts looking for information on American Indian pottery he is faced with one of two dilemmas: 1) there is nothing available or 2) there is too much. This bibliography, it is hoped, will help him steer a course between the two extremes.

The compiler is not an archaeologist nor an anthropologist and can claim to be only a very amateur collector, but twenty-five years in the library profession, many of which were spent in special Southwest collections, have given him some experience in bibliographic methods. This work grew over the years from material collected while helping library patrons pursue their interest in the subject. It is designed for the beginner and the layman. No highly specialized archaeological collections were consulted. Most of the material was found in public and university libraries.

The American Southwest in this work has been limited generally to New Mexico and Arizona though references will be found to Southern California, Utah, Colorado, Texas, and Northern Mexico. The entries have been divided into three sections:

General—books and articles on the history, archaeology, anthropology and culture of Southwestern Indians. The items are not specifically about pottery, but all contain some information on the subject.

Prehistoric—all entries concern Southwestern pottery before the advent of Europeans, roughly through the sixteenth century.

Historic—pottery after the Spanish conquest, seventeenth century to date.

This is a somewhat selective bibliography. For every item used four or five were discarded and probably ten or more were missed. The ones found here have proved useful to others and should act as a good base for the beginner.

Note: BAE is the abbreviation for the Bureau of American Ethnology.

GENERAL

ALEXANDER, HARTLEY BURR. *L'art et la philosophie des Indiens de l'Amerique du Nord.* Paris: Editions Ernest Leroux, 1926.

AMSDEN, CHARLES AVERY. *Prehistoric Southwesterners from Basketmaker to Pueblo.* Los Angeles: Southwest Museum, 1949.

APPLETON, LEROY H. *Indian art of the Americas.* New York: Scribners, 1950.

BAHTI, TOM. *An introduction to Southwestern Indian arts and crafts.* Flagstaff, Ariz.: KD Publications, 1964.

BALDWIN, GORDON CORTIS. *The ancient ones: Basketmakers and cliff dwellers of the Southwest.* New York: Norton, 1963.

BOAS, FRANZ. "The decorative art of the North American Indians." *Popular Science Monthly*, Oct. 1903.

_____. *Primitive art.* Cambridge, Mass.: 1927.

COOLIDGE, DANE and COOLIDGE, MARY R. *The Navajo Indians.* Boston: Houghton Mifflin, 1930.

CURTIS, EDWARD S. *The North American Indian.* ed. by F. W. Hodge. 20 v. New York: Johnson Reprint Corp., 1970 (1907-30)

DE HUFF, ELIZABETH W. *Swift-Eagle of the Rio Grande.* Chicago: Rand McNally, 1928.

DOUGLAS, FREDERIC H. *Indian design series.* Denver: Denver Art Museum, Department of Indian Art, 1933-34.

DOUGLAS, FREDERIC H. and D'HARNONCOURT, RENE. *Indian art of the United States.* New York: 1941.

FEDER, NORMAN. *Two hundred years of North American Indian Art.* New York: Praeger, 1972.

GLADWIN, HAROLD S. *A history of the ancient Southwest.* Portland, Me.: Bond Wheelwright, 1957.

GODDARD, PLINY EARLE. *Indians of the Southwest.* New York: 1931.

HARTT, CHARLES F. *Notes on the manufacture of pottery among savage races.* Boston: 1897.
(Note: from *American Naturalist*, February, 1879. Listed in *Dictionary Catalog of the Edward E. Ayer Collection of Americana and American Indians in the Newberry Library*)

HEWETT, EDGAR L. *Ancient life in the American Southwest.* Indianapolis: Bobbs-Merrill, 1930

HODGE, FREDERICK W. *Handbook of American Indians north of Mexico.* 2 v. BAE Bulletin no. 30. Washington, D. C.: 1907-10.

HOLMES, WILLIAM H. "Origin and development of form and ornament in ceramic art." *BAE, Annual report,* 4th. pp. 437-65. Washington, D.C.: 1886.

JAMES, GEORGE WHARTON. *A little journey to New Mexico and Arizona.* Chicago: Flanagan, 1930.

JAMES, H. L. *Acoma, people of the White Rock.* Glorieta, N.M.: Rio Grande Press, 1970.

KIDDER, ALFRED V. *An introduction to the study of Southwestern archaeology, with a preliminary account of the excavations at Pecos, New Mexico.* New Haven: 1924.

KLUCKHOHN, CLYDE; HILL, W. W. and KLUCKHOHN, LUCY WALES. *Navaho material culture.* Cambridge: The Belknap Press of Harvard University Press, 1971.

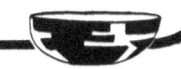

McGREGOR, JOHN C. *Southwestern archaeology.* New York: Wiley, 1941.

MARRIOTT, ALICE and RACHLIN, CAROL K. *American epic, the story of the American Indian.* New York: Putnam, 1969.

NORDENSKEOLD, G. *The cliff dwellers of the Mesa Verde.* Stockholm: 1893.

OTIS, RAYMOND. *Indian art of the Southwest.* Santa Fe: Southwest Indian Fair, 1931.

RUSSELL, FRANK. "The Pima Indians." *BAE Annual report,* 26th. pp. 3-389. Washington, D. C.: 1908.

SCHOOL ARTS MAGAZINE. Special Indian Numbers. November, 1927; March, 1931.

SHEPARD, ANNA O. *Ceramics for the archaeologist.* Carnegie Institution of Washington Publication 609. Washington, D.C.: 1956.

SIDES, DOROTHY SMITH. *Decorative art of the Southwestern Indians.* New York: Dover, 1961.

SLOAN, JOHN and LA FARGE, OLIVER. *Introduction to American Indian art.* New York: 1931.

STEVENSON, MATILDA COXE. "The Sia." *BAE, Annual report,* 11th. pp. 3-157. Washington, D.C.: 1894.

——————. "The Zuni Indians.::

——————. "The Zuni Indians." *BAE' ANN*

——————. "The Zuni Indians." *BAE, Annual report,* 23d. Washington, D.C.: 1901-2.

UNDERHILL, RUTH. *Pueblo crafts.* Lawrence, Kans.: Haskell Institute, 1944.

U. S. OFFICE OF INDIAN AFFAIRS. *Indian art and industries.* Chilocco: Indian Print Shop, 1927.

VAILLANT, GEORGE C. *Indian arts of North America.* New York: 1939.

WESTLAKE, INEZ B. *American Indian designs.* 1st series. New York: Perleberg, 1925.

_____ . _____ . 2d series. Philadelphia: Perleberg, 1930.

WHITE, LESLIE A. *The Pueblo of Sia, New Mexico.* BAE Bulletin no. 184. Washington, D. C.: 1962.

WISSLER, CLARK. *Indians of the U.S.* American Museum of Natural History. Science Series. New York: Doubleday, Doran, 1940.

PREHISTORIC

ABEL, LELAND L. "Wares 5A, 10A, 10B, and 12A." *Pottery types of the Southwest,* Ceramic Series no. 3. Flagstaff: Museum of Northern Arizona, 1955.

AMSDEN, CHARLES A. *An analysis of Hohokam pottery design.* Medallion Papers no. 23. Globe, Ariz.: Privately printed, 1936.

_____ . "The Pinto Basin artifacts." In E.W.C. and H.W. Campbell, *The Pinto Basin site.* Southwest Museum Papers no. 9, pp. 33-51. Los Angeles: 1935.

BRAND, DONALD. "The distribution of pottery types in Northwest Mexico," *American Anthropologist* 37 (1935): 287-305.

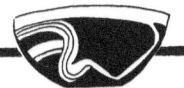

BRETERNITZ, DAVID A. *An appraisal of tree-ring dated pottery in the Southwest.* Anthropological Papers of the University of Arizona no. 10. Tucson: 1966.

BRUGGE, DAVID M. *Navajo pottery and ethnohistory.* Navajo publications, series 2. Window Rock, Ariz.: Navajo Tribal Museum, 1963.

BUSHNELL, GEOFFREY H.S. and DIGBY, ADRIAN. *Ancient American pottery.* The Faber monographs on pottery and porcelain. New York: Pitman, 1955.

CASSIDY, FRANCIS E. "Navajo remains in New Mexico." In *Pipeline Archaeology.* Santa Fe and Flagstaff: Museum of New Mexico and Museum of Northern Arizona, 1956.

CLARKE, ELEANOR P. *Designs on the prehistoric pottery of Arizona.* University of Arizona Bulletin no. 9 (Social Science Bulletin vol. VI, no. 4) Tucson: University of Arizona Press, 1935.

COLTON, HAROLD S. *An archaeological survey of Northwestern Arizona including the description of fifteen new pottery types.* Museum of Northern Arizona Bulletin no. 16. Flagstaff: Northern Arizona Society of Science and Art, 1939.

_____ . *Potsherds.* Museum of Northern Arizona Bulletin no. 25. Flagstaff: Northern Arizona Society of Science and Art, 1953.

COLTON, HAROLD S. and HARGRAVE, LYNDON. *Handbook of Northern Arizona pottery wares.* Museum of Northern Arizona Bulletin no. 11. Flagstaff: Northern Arizona Society of Science and Art, 1937.

DANSON, EDWARD BRIDGE. "An archaeological survey of West Central New Mexico and East Central Arizona." *Papers of the Peabody Museum of Archaeology and Ethnology* vol. XLIV, no. 1. Cambridge, Mass.: 1957.

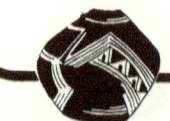

DANSON, EDWARD BRIDGE and WALLACE, R. M. "A petrographic study of Gila polychrome." *American Antiquity* 22 (1956): 180-83.

FEWKES, JESSE WALTER. *Additional designs on prehistoric Mimbres pottery.* Washington, D. C.: Smithsonian Institution, 1924.

_____. *Ancient Zuni pottery.* Putnam Anniversary volume, pp. 43-82. New York: 1909.

_____. "Animal figures on prehistoric pottery from Mimbres Valley, New Mexico." *American Anthropologist, n.s.* 18:4 (1916)

_____. *Antiquities of Mesa Verde National Park, Cliff Palace.* BAE Bulletin no. 51. Washington, D. C.: 1911.

_____. *Antiquities of Mesa Verde National Park, Spruce Tree House.* BAE Bulletin no. 41. Washington, D. C.: 1909.

_____. "Antiquities of the upper Verde River and Walnut Creek Valleys, Arizona." *BAE, Annual report,* 28th. pp. 181-220. Washington, D. C.: 1912.

_____. "Archaeological expedition to Arizona in 1895." *BAE, Annual report,* 17th, pt. 2. pp. 519-742. Washington, D. C.: 1898.

_____. "Casa Grande, Arizona." *BAE, Annual report,* 28th. pp. 25-197. Washington, D. C.: 1912.

_____. "Designs on prehistoric Hopi pottery." *BAE, Annual report,* 33d. pp. 207-284. Washington, D. C.: 1919.

_____. "Designs on prehistoric pottery from Mimbres Valley, New Mexico." *Smithsonian Miscellaneous Collections,* v. 74, no. 6. Washington, D. C.: 1923.

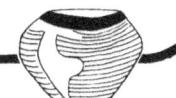

_____. "Two summers' work in Pueblo ruins." *BAE, Annual report,* 22d. pp. 1-195. Washington, D. C.: 1904.

_____. *Preliminary report on a visit to the Navaho National monument, Arizona.* BAE Bulletin no. 50. Washington, D. C.: 1911.

GIFFORD, JAMES C. "A guide to the description of pottery types in the Southwest." Mimeographed. Tucson: University of Arizona, 1953.

GLADWIN, HAROLD S. *A method for the designation of Southwestern pottery types.* Globe, Ariz.: 1930.

_____. *Red-on-buff culture of the Gila Basin.* Pasadena, Calif.: 1929.

_____. *The use of potsherds in an archaeological survey of the Southwest.* Pasadena, Calif.: 1928.

GLADWIN, HAROLD S. and GLADWIN, WINIFRED. *The red-on-buff culture of the Papagueria.* Medallion Papers no. 4. Globe, Ariz.: 1929.

_____. *Some Southwestern pottery types, series III.* Medallion Papers no. 13. Globe, Ariz.: 1933.

_____. *The western range of the red-on-buff culture.* Medallion Papers no. 5. Globe, Ariz.: 1930.

GLADWIN, NORA. "Petrography of Snaketown pottery." In H. S. Gladwin et al, *Excavations at Snaketown: Material Culture.* pp. 230-32. Medallion Papers no. 25. Tucson: Reprinted for Arizona State Museum by University of Arizona Press, 1938, 1965.

GLADWIN, WINIFRED and GLADWIN, HAROLD S. *Some Southwestern pottery types, series II.* Medallion Papers no. 10. Globe, Ariz.: 1931.

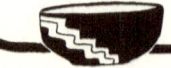

HALES, HENRY. "Prehistoric New Mexican pottery." *Smithsonian Institution, Annual report, 1892.* pp. 535-54. Washington, D.C.: 1893.

HAMMACK, LAURENS C. "Effigy vessels in the prehistoric American Southwest." *Arizona Highways* 50:2 (1974): 33-37.

HARGRAVE, L. L. *Guide to forty pottery types from Hopi country and the San Francisco Mountains.* Museum of Northern Arizona Bulletin 1. Flagstaff: 1932.

HARRINGTON, JOHN PEABODY. "The ethnogeography of the Tewa Indians." *BAE, Annual report,* 29th. pp.29-636. Washington, D. C.: 1916.

HATT, GUDMUND. "Notes on the archaeology of the Santo Domingo." *Geografisk tidsskrift.* 35. bindl 1./2. hefte (1932): 9-21.

HAURY, EMIL W. "Figurines and miscellaneous clay objects." In H. S. Gladwin et al, *Excavations at Snaketown: Material Culture.* pp. 233-45. Medallion Papers no. 25. Tucson: reprinted for Arizona State Museum by University of Arizona Press, 1938, 1965.

_____. "Pottery types at Snaketown." In H. S. Gladwin et al, *Excavations at Snaketown: Material Culture.* pp. 169-228. Medallion Papers No. 25. Tucson: reprinted for Arizona State Museum by University of Arizona Press, 1938, 1965.

_____. *Some Southwestern pottery types, series IV.* Medallion Papers no. 19. Globe, Ariz.: 1936.

HAWLEY, FLORENCE M. "Additions to descriptions of Chaco pottery types." In C. Kluckhohn and P. Reiter, eds., *Preliminary report on the 1937 excavations, Bc50-51, Chaco Canyon, New Mexico.* pp. 49-53. University of New Mexico Bulletin, Anthropological series vol. 3, no. 2. Albuquerque: 1939.

_____. *Classification of black pottery pigments and paint areas.* University of New Mexico Bulletin, Anthropological series vol. 2, no. 4. Albuquerque: 1938.

_____. *Field manual of prehistoric pottery types.* University of New Mexico Bulletin, Anthropological series vol. 1, no. 4 (rev.). Albuquerque: 1950.

_____. "Prehistoric pottery pigments in the Southwest." *American Anthropologist, n.s.* 31 (1929): 731-54.

HEWETT, EDGAR L. *Antiquities of the Jemez Plateau, New Mexico.* BAE Bulletin no. 32. Washington, D. C.: 1906.

_____. *Pajarito Plateau and its ancient people.* Handbooks of archaeological history. Albuquerque: University of New Mexico Press, 1938.

HODGE, FREDERICK W. *Pottery of Hawikuh.* Indian Notes. New York: Museum of the American Indian, Heye Foundation, 1924.

HOLMES, WILLIAM H. "Illustrated catalogue of a portion of the collections made by the Bureau of Ethnology during field season of 1881." *BAE, Annual report,* 3d. pp. 427-510. Washington, D. C.: 1884.

_____. "Pottery of the ancient Pueblos." *BAE, Annual report,* 4th. pp. 257-360. Washington, D. C.: 1886.

HOUGH, WALTER. *Antiquities of Upper Gila and Salt River valleys in Arizona and New Mexico.* BAE Bulletin no. 35. Washington, D. C.: 1907.

HUSCHER, BETTY H. and HUSCHER, HAROLD A. "Potsherds from a Pinyon Tree!" *The Masterkey* 14:4 (1940)

JUDD, N.M. *The material culture of Pueblo Bonito.* Smithsonian Miscellaneous Collection vol. 124. Washington, D. C.:1954.

KIDDER, ALFRED V. *The pottery of Casas Grandes District, Chihuahua.* Holmes Anniversary Volume, pp. 253-68. Washington, D.C.: 1916.

_____. *Pottery of Pecos.* v. 1. New Haven: Yale University Press, 1931.

_____. *Pottery of the Pajarito Plateau and of some adjacent regions in New Mexico.* Lancaster, Pa.: American Anthropological Association, 1915.

KIDDER, ALFRED V. and KIDDER, M. A. "Notes on the pottery of Pecos." *American Anthropologist, n.s.* 19 (1917): 325-60.

KROEBER, ALFRED L. *Zuni potsherds.* New York: American Museum of Natural History, 1916.

KROEBER, ALFRED L. and HARNER, MICHAEL J. "Mohave pottery." *Anthropological Records* 16 (1955).

LAMBERT, MARJORIE F. *Paa-Ko, archaeological chronicle of an Indian village in North Central New Mexico,* pts. I-V. School of American Research Monograph 19, pts. I-V. Santa Fe: 1954.

LAMBERT, MARJORIE F. and AMBLER, J. RICHARD. *A survey and excavation of caves in Hidalgo County, New Mexico.* School of American Research Monograph 25. Santa Fe: 1965.

MERA, HARRY PERCIVAL. *Ceramic clues to the prehistory of North Central New Mexico.* Laboratory of Anthropology, Technical Series, Bulletin no. 8. Santa Fe: 1935.

_____. *An outline of ceramic developments in Southern and Southeastern New Mexico.* Laboratory of Anthropology, Technical Series, Bulletin no. 11. Santa Fe: 1943.

_____. *A proposed revision of the Rio Grande glaze paint sequence.* Laboratory of Anthropology, Archaeological Survey, Technical Series, Bulletin no. 5. Santa Fe: 1933.

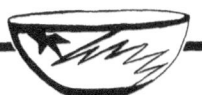

_____ . *A survey of the biscuit ware area in Northern New Mexico.* Laboratory of Anthropology, Archaeological Survey, Technical Series, Bulletin no. 6. Santa Fe: 1934.

_____ . *Wares ancestral to Tewa polychrome.* Laboratory of Anthropology, Archaeological Survey, Technical Series, Bulletin no. 4. Santa Fe: 1932.

MERA, HARRY PERCIVAL and STALLINGS, W. S. Jr. *Lincoln black-on-red.* Laboratory of Anthropology, Archaeological Survey, Technical Series, Bulletin no. 2. Santa Fe: 1931.

MINNEAPOLIS INSTITUTE OF ARTS. "The Mimbres Valley Expedition." *Minneapolis Institute of Arts Bulletin* 17:31 (1928)

MORRIS, EARL H. *The beginnings of pottery making in the San Juan area.* New York: American Museum of Natural History, 1927.

MORSS, NOEL. *Clay figurines of the American Southwest.* Papers of the Peabody Museum of Archaeology and Ethnology, vol. 49, no. 1. Cambridge: Harvard University Press, 1954.

NESBITT, PAUL HOMER. *The ancient Mimbrenos, based on investigations at the Mattocks ruin, Mimbres Valley, New Mexico.* Logan Museum Bulletin no. 4. Beloit, Wis.: 1931.

NETTLE, ELEANOR JANE. "Portable material culture, LA4070 and LA4363." In J. Schoenwetter and F. W. Eddy, *Alluvial and palynological reconstruction of environments, Navajo Reservoir District.* pp. 129-49. Museum of New Mexico Papers in Anthropology no. 13. Santa Fe: 1964.

ORCHARD, WILLIAM C. *Fine line decoration of ancient Southwestern pottery.* Indian Notes. New York: Museum of the American Indian, Heye Foundation, 1925.

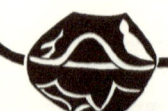

PEPPER, GEORGE H. *Pueblo Bonito.* Anthropological Papers of the American Museum of Natural History, vol. 27. New York: 1920.

PILLES, PETER J. and DANSON, EDWARD B. "The prehistoric pottery of Arizona." *Arizona Highways* 50:2 (1974):2-5.

PUEBLO GRANDE ARCHAEOLOGICAL RUINS, MUSEUM, AND LABORATORY, PHOENIX, ARIZONA. *Prehistoric Hohokam pottery designs from the Salt River Valley, Arizona.* Phoenix: 1941.

REED, ERIK K. "Painted pottery and Zuni history." *Southwestern Journal of Anthropology* 11 (1955): 178-93.

_____. "Pottery types of the Manuelito District." *American Antiquity* 10:2 (1944)

RENAUD, E.-B. *Les origines de la ceramique indienne du Sud-Ouest Americain.* Paris: 1928.

RINALDO, JOHN. "Pottery." In P.S. Martin, *The Su Site, excavations at a Mogollon village, Western New Mexico, 1939.* pp. 78-84. Chicago: Kraus Reprint, 1968.

RINALDO, JOHN BEACH and BLUHM, ELAINE A. "Late Mogollon pottery types of the Reserve area." *Chicago Natural History Museum. Fieldiana: Anthropology* 36 (1956): 149-87.

ROBERTS, FRANK H. H. Jr. *Early Pueblo ruins in the Piedra District, Southwestern Colorado.* BAE Bulletin no. 96. Washington, D.C.: 1930.

_____. *The village of the Great Kivas on the Zuni reservation, New Mexico.* BAE Bulletin no. 11. Washington, D.C.: 1932.

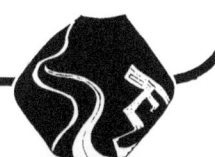

ROGERS, MALCOLM J. "Yuman pottery making." *San Diego Museum Papers* no. 2 (1936)

SAYLES, E. B. *Some Southwestern pottery types, Series V.* Medallion Papers no. 21. Globe, Ariz.: 1936.

SCANTLING, FREDERICK H. "The bearing of ceramics on development in the Hohokam classic period." *Southwest Journal of Anthropology* 8 (1952): 320-34.

_____. "Comments on Gila polychrome." *American Antiquity* 23 (1957): 169-70.

SCHMIDT, ERICH F. *Time-relations of prehistoric pottery types in southern Arizona.* American Museum of Natural History Anthropological papers, vol. XXX, pt. V. New York: 1928.

SHEPARD, ANNA O. "Rio Grande glaze paint ware: a study illustrating the place of ceramic technological analysis in archaeological research." In *Carnegie Institution of Washington, Contributions to American anthropology and history,* no. 39. Washington, D.C.: 1942.

_____. "Technological observations on the later black-on-white pottery from Site 34." In D. O'Bryan, *Excavations in Mesa Verde National Park, 1947-1948.* pp. 93-98. Medallion Papers no. 39. Globe, Ariz.: 1950.

_____. "Technology of La Plata pottery." In E. H. Morris, *Archaeological studies in the La Plata district, Southwestern Colorado and Northwestern New Mexico.* pp. 249-98. Carnegie Institution of Washington, Publication 519. Washington, D.C.: 1939.

SPIER, LESLIE. "An outline for a chronology of Zuni ruins." *Anthropological Papers,* American Museum of Natural History, vol. XVIII, pt. e. New York: 1917.

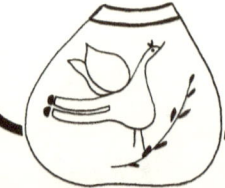

STALLINGS, W. S. Jr. *El Paso polychrome.* Laboratory of Anthropology, Technical Series, Bulletin no. 3. Santa Fe: 1931.

WENDORF, FRED; FOX, NANCY and LEWIS, ORIAN L., eds. *Pipeline archaeology, reports of salvage operations in the Southwest on El Paso Natural Gas Company Projects 1950 1953.* Santa Fe and Flagstaff: The Laboratory of Anthropology and The Museum of Northern Arizona, 1956.

WENDORF, FRED. *Salvage archaeology in the Chama Valley, New Mexico.* School of American Research Monograph 17. Santa Fe: 1953.

HISTORIC

ARIZONA HIGHWAYS (entire issue) 50:5 (1974)

AUSTIN, MARY. *Indian pottery of the Rio Grande.* Pasadena: Esto Pub. Co., 1934.

BUNZEL, RUTH. *The Pueblo potter.* New York: Columbia University Press, 1929.

CHAPMAN, KENNETH M. "Post-Spanish Pueblo pottery." *Art and Archaeology* 23 (1927): 207-13.

_____. *The pottery of San Ildefonso.* Supplementary text by F. H. Harlow. SAR Monograph Series no. 28. Albuquerque: for School of American Research by University of New Mexico Press, 1970.

_____. *The pottery of Santo Domingo.* Memoirs of the Laboratory of Anthropology. Santa Fe: 1938.

_____. *Pueblo Indian pottery*, part 1. Nice, France: C. Szwedzicki, 1933.

_____. *Pueblo pottery of the post-Spanish period.* Laboratory of Anthropology, General Series, Bulletin no. 4. Santa Fe: 1938.

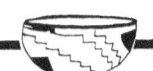

CHAPMAN, KENNETH M. and ELLIS, BRUCE T. "The line break, problem child of Pueblo pottery." *El Palacio* 58 (1951): 251-89.

CUSHING, FRANK HAMILTON. "A study of Pueblo pottery as illustrative of Zuni culture growth." *BAE, Annual report,* 4th. pp. 467-521. Washington, D.C.: 1886.

_____. *Zuni breadstuff.* New York: Heye Foundation, Museum of the American Indian, 1920.

_____. "Zuni fetishes." *BAE, Annual report,* 2d. pp. 3-45. Washington, D. C.: 1883.

DOBYNS, HENRY F. "A Mohave potter's experiment." *The Kiva* 24 (1959):16.

DOUGLAS, FREDERIC H. *Modern Pueblo pottery types.* Leaflets no. 53-54. Denver: Denver Art Museum, Department of Indian Art, 1933.

_____. *Seven Navajo pots.* Material Culture Notes no. 3. Denver: Denver Art Museum, 1937.

DOUGLAS, FREDERIC H. and RAYNOLDS, F. R. "Pottery design terminology." *Newsletter,* Clearing House for Southwestern Museums 35 (1941)

DUMAREST, NOEL. *Notes on Cochiti, New Mexico.* Lancaster, Pa.: American Anthropological Association, 1919.

FEWKES, JESSE W. "Clay figurines made by Navajo children." *American Anthropologist* 25 (1923): 559-63.

FONTANA, BERNARD L.; ROBINSON, W. J., et al. *Papago Indian pottery.* The American Ethnological Society. Seattle: University of Washington Press, 1962.

FRANK, LARRY and HARLOW, FRANCIS H. *Historic pottery of the Pueblo Indians, 1600-1880.* Boston: New York Graphic Society, 1974.

GERALD, REX E. "A description of an historic Papago redware and its comparison with other later redwares." unpublished manuscript. Tucson: Department of Anthropology, University of Arizona, 1951.

GIFFORD, E. W. *Pottery-making in the Southwest.* Publications in American archaeology and ethnology vol. 23, pp. 353-73. Berkeley: University of California, 1928.

GODDARD, PLINY EARLE. *Pottery of the Southwestern Indians.* New York: American Museum of Natural History, 1931.

GUTHE, CARL E. *Pueblo pottery making, a study at the village of San Ildefonso.* Papers of the Phillips Academy Southwestern Expedition no. 2. New Haven: Yale University Press, 1925.

HARLOW, FRANCIS H. *Matte-paint pottery of the Tewa, Keres, and Zuni Pueblos.* Santa Fe: Museum of New Mexico, 1973.

HAYDEN, JULIAN D. "Notes on Pima pottery making." *The Kiva* 24 (1959):10-16.

HEWETT, EDGAR L. *Native American artists.* Washington, D.C.: Washington Archaeological Society, 1922.

HILL, GERTRUDE. "Notes on Papago pottery manufacture at Santa Rosa, Arizona." *American Anthropologist* 44 (1942): 531-33.

HILL, W. W. *Navajo pottery manufacture.* University of New Mexico Bulletin, Anthropological Series vol. 2, no. 3. Albuquerque: 1937.

21

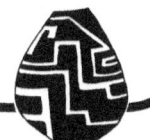

HIRN, YRJÖ. *Skildringar ur pueblofolkens konstlif.* Helsingfors: Helsingfors centraltryckeri, 1901.

HOUGH, WALTER. *The Hopi Indian collection in the U.S. National Museum.* Washington, D.C.: Smithsonian Institution, 1918.

HYDE, HAZEL. *Maria making pottery.* Santa Fe: Sunstone Press, 1973.

JAMES, MARJORIE. "A note on Navajo pottery making." *El Palacio* 43 (1937):85-86.

LEFREE, BETTY. *Santa Clara pottery: the story of an ancient craft.* Albuquerque: University of New Mexico Press, 1974.

MARRIOTT, ALICE. *Maria, the potter of San Ildefonso.* Civilization of the American Indian. Norman: University of Oklahoma Press, 1948.

MERA, HARRY PERCIVAL. *Pueblo designs: "The Rain Bird."* 2 vols. Reprint (vol. 1) New York: Dover, 1971.

_____. *The "rain bird": a study in Pueblo design.* Laboratory of Anthropology, Memoirs vol. 2. Santa Fe: 1937.

_____. *Style trends of Pueblo pottery in the Rio Grande and Little Colorado cultural areas from the sixteenth to the nineteenth century.* Laboratory of Anthropology, Memoirs vol. 3. Santa Fe: 1939.

PARSONS, ELSIE CLEWS. "Isleta, New Mexico." *BAE, Annual report,* 47th. pp. 193-466. Washington, D.C.: 1932.

SAUNDERS, CHARLES FRANCIS. "The ceramic art of the Pueblo Indians." *International Studio* 41 (1910): 56-70.

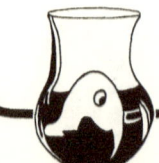

SAYLES, GLADYS and SAYLES, TED. "The pottery of Ida Redbird." *Arizona Highways* 24(1948):28-31.

STEVENSON, JAMES. "Illustrated catalogue of collections obtained from Indians of New Mexico and Arizona in 1879." *BAE, Annual report,* 2d. pp. 307-422. Washington, D.C.: 1883.

_____. "Illustrated catalogue of the collection obtained from the Indians of New Mexico in 1880." *BAE, Annual report,* 2d. pp. 423-65. Washington, D.C.: 1883.

_____. "Illustrated catalogue of the collections obtained from the Pueblos of Zuni, New Mexico, and Walpi, Arizona, in 1881." *BAE, Annual report,* 3d. pp. 511-14. Washington, D.C.: 1884.

TSCHOPIK, HARRY S. Jr. *Navaho pottery making; an inquiry into the affinities of Navaho painted pottery.* Papers of the Peabody Museum of American Archaeology and Ethnology vol. 17, no. 1. Cambridge: Harvard University, 1941.

_____. "Taboo as a possible factor involved in the obsolescence of Navaho pottery and basketry." *American Anthropologist* 40 (1938):257-62.

WARD, BOB. "Pueblo pottery." *New Mexico Magazine* 52:5-6 (1974):23-30.

WORMINGTON, H.M. and ARMINTA, NEAL. *The story of Pueblo pottery.* Museum Pictorial no. 2. Denver: Denver Museum of Natural History, 1951.

ADDENDA

FRANK, LARRY and HARLOW, FRANCIS H. "Historic Pottery of the Pueblo Indians, 1600-1880." Boston: New York Graphic Society, 1974.

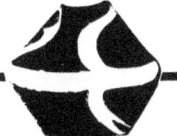

ADDITIONAL SOURCES

For those wishing to study Southwestern American Indian pottery further, the following series of publications are suggested. Not all publications in these series are devoted to pottery but a quick perusal of the contents will show the reader what is available.

MUSEUM OF NEW MEXICO, Santa Fe. *Papers in Anthropology.*

LABORATORY OF ANTHROPOLOGY, MUSEUM OF NEW MEXICO, Santa Fe. All series.

SCHOOL OF AMERICAN RESEARCH, Santa Fe. All series.

CHICAGO NATURAL HISTORY MUSEUM. *Fieldiana: Anthropology Series.*

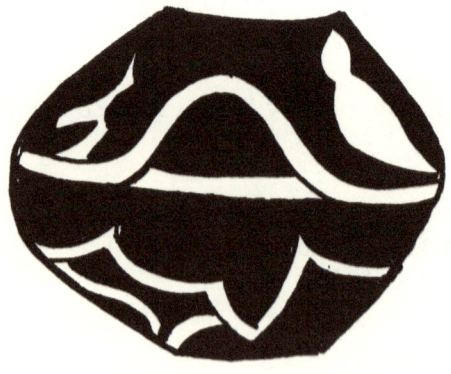

www.ingramcontent.com/pod-product-compliance
Lightning Source LLC
Chambersburg PA
CBHW020333290526
45785CB00007B/3049